GW00731310

For Sebastian, Sophie and Charlotte

DEDICATION

A book of my wishes for you, my darling Sebastian. Delivered, not as orders but as road signs to point you in a new direction.

I wish for you to feel my words like a loving hug any time you need one but particularly if the route you are travelling is taking you away from your destination.

Written with the smallest of you in my mind but with all of you in my heart.

ISBN: 9798503790191

CONTENTS

1 Introduction

Throughout my eventful and colourful life, whatever the situation, if there is something I need to talk about or I feel I need advice, I call my mum. From the top of a mountain to the depths of a submarine, from times of overwhelming fear to moments of great joy, I share my life and questions with her. I hope you will do the same with me and in realising that mums can sometimes be busy (let's hope that I am regularly found on a long-haul flight or relaxing in an exotic and faraway land), this book is intended to be a guide to refer to if you need a helping hand and I simply cannot answer the phone.

In so many ways, we are alike; our hair, our eyes, our noses, the way we laugh, how we react in many situations – when you were small, we would often knowingly look each other in the eye and say 'we're the same' or 'snap.'

These moments were special, but, I do realise that you are your own person with your own ideas and ideals. Therefore, it would be amiss of me not to use this book as a way of directing you back to your unique innate qualities. To remind you of your natural reactions, the instinctive parts of you that were there way before the big, wide world tries to weave its way in.

Please be assured, this is absolutely *not* a book of orders. I don't have all the answers and I am far from having all this stuff figured out. That said, whilst we are here, I hold faith that what I have written will resonate with you and hopefully guide you in times of need or self-doubt.

I hope that some of my calmness remains with you but more than that, I simply wish for you to be you, to continue to be instinctively kind, honorable, honest and loyal.

I wish for you to dream big, follow your dreams, eat cake, don't eat too much cake and eat your greens (even if it is still just cucumber!). From someone who knows first-hand, do not underestimate the importance of sleep, throw yourself into a fun hobby, be careful, be fearless, travel often and be mindful of the environment - you get the picture.

Most of this book focuses on work and the life lessons I have learned along the way. My career has been a big part of my life. That said, the insights, encouragement, and wisdom I share within these pages are for you to take as you wish, which areas of your life you choose to apply them to is for you to decide, for your path is yours to tread.

My own journey has been mostly fearless, a leap from adventures to opportunities of deep learning. I have experienced some unforgettable, life-changing, happy tear-evoking moments along the way. As well as my career, my happy and supportive marriage to your dad has been a noted triumph.

Your Granny once told me on the night before my wedding day that I was in for a "lifetime of fun" - and as you well know, your Granny is always right!

Please understand my intentions of this book and of my wishes for you. Remember;

It's not your duty to make me happy.
It's not your job to do as I say or follow my wishes.
It's not up to me, or anybody else for that matter to choose
how you live your life or the direction you travel.

Of course, even with this in mind, I hope you choose to stay within the law, remain respectful of society and do not put anyone's safety, including your own, at unnecessary risk. That a given, I see it as my job as your parent to help guide you to make good choices and to be well equipped to face the world, I hope with an understanding of how you can live a peaceful, fulfilled life.

This guidance is a loose extension of how your Grandpa used to declare, every year (without fail), his New Year's resolution as: 'no regrets'. He would say this with a knowing twinkle in his eyes, like he was the keeper of this mysterious secret that held the answer to all New Year's reflections. He is a very wise man but, in my youth, I wondered what on earth he meant. Now though I know what he knew all along, there should never be space taken up with regret, all space should be saved for the now. Take the lesson, commit it to your intellect and move forward, looking behind you means, unless you want to go backwards, you cannot actually see where you are going. You see, I told you he was wise!

I succeeded
I broke
I didn't learn
I grew
I learned
I realised

And, now I wish for you to realise sooner than I did. My shift in understanding could have been more useful to your sisters when they came into my care. I have no regrets, I simply didn't know but, now that I do, hopefully these words will touch them too and anyone else who chooses to read this book.

You are perfect

Exactly as you are.

What is success?

The younger me used to think success was measured by the challenges I overcame, the fear and vulnerability I didn't show to my peers, the exciting stories I could share. I would channel my energy into keeping up appearances, which is exhausting, presenting a version of myself that was bolder, stronger, braver than the last. Please don't feel sorry for me, I enjoyed my life. In my career I travelled the world, I negotiated groundbreaking deals, I was a significant part of important teams delivering vital and interesting projects – I got a buzz out of accomplishing great things and recognising my achievements.

In my personal life, I had fun too, but I now realise that too much a part of me took validation from other people. When I was younger, like most youngsters in the western world, I wanted to look and act the part and often put my own needs beneath the needs of those around me, way down at the bottom of the pile and this stuck for too long. I mistakenly thought that if everybody else's needs were met, I was doing a good job.

Always seeking the better contract, the bigger deal, the more challenging role whilst at the same time running around desperately trying to keep everybody else happy took its toll – I felt like an elastic band stretched so far and so wide that eventually, I snapped.

I operated in the alpha state, my mind in a constant flux of flight or fight - ready to protect me from the next threat - be it personal or corporate. I fed this state with an unhealthy mix of processed food diet and late-night drinking, never allowing my frazzled state to calm. I attributed my worth to how stressful my job role was. I thought this stress was a good thing, that it was what kept me going, - I could handle it, I thought this was who I was, what made me, me.

My own wellbeing, understanding my true self beneath all this activity was not even a consideration. I became lost.

Sadly, the first thing to go missing was joy. As time passed, I laughed less and less. I forgot what I enjoyed. If I ever slowed down for long enough to wonder 'what do I love', I would have absolutely no clue what the answer was. My pre-programmed reaction would be 'opportunity' and to a degree, this is still true, I do indeed love the thrill of seeking out something new, focusing on making things happen, but that does not answer the question of what do I do for joy, with no expectation or goal, just pure enjoyment.

Next, I became bitter. I focused my thinking on the people and circumstances around me that I believed caused me to feel so lost. My mind was racing with judgement and negativity, walking around internally tutting at everyone and everything. I saw no good in situations, only blame and lack. I treated myself like a victim.

I couldn't sleep, I would toss and turn with blame, criticising other people's actions, believing how I was feeling was their fault. I couldn't let it go. As an attempt at distraction, I would scroll on my phone into the early hours, self-diagnosing minor ailments or staring for something to take me away from the battle in my head. I was exhausted, compounding my low mood.

Then, the dread.

I dreaded work, my commute, people, mindless conversations, and small talk.

I dreaded being found out for being weak, for not holding it together or my happy mask slipping off and for not being the person I always thought I was.

For that matter, who even was I?

This situation led me to spiral down to my lowest point and from there I began a transformation - a journey of discovery, learning and finding new meaning. Don't worry, I didn't become a hippy or join a cult, but I was pointed in a new direction and, through several sources, I realised there is a better way.

Now I know, to me success is peace. Peace of mind, enjoying a peaceful home and preserving peaceful, yet supportive relationships. Once I realised this and re-focused, everything else fitted into place around me.

It still amazes me that, even with this understanding, I didn't actually have to change a single thing in my life, I just choose to approach situations in a different way. I didn't take time off work, I didn't have to have difficult conversations with family, I just learned to get out of my own head and lead my life from my heart.

2 A life of SECURITY

You are exactly where you are meant to be - always

When I met your dad, I was 28 and had what I called the 'best job in the world'. As the International Development Director of a logistics company, I travelled negotiating deals and was happily making many, many memories. I got myself into some scrapes, but I was also good at my job. You might think this sounds like I have a big ego, but this is not what I intend to get across, I am just not ashamed to own my strengths.

Flying high, as I was, the timing wasn't right for me to think about having a family of my own, but I hadn't ruled the option out. Your dad was, however, already a loving father to your two wonderful sisters, Charlotte and Sophie. At that time, there was a lot already going on in the separate lives that our very new relationship brought together, and with so much to focus on, your dad wasn't initially open to the option of having more children.

Whilst being with your dad meant I had 'inherited' an eight- and 10-year-old, I didn't want the option of having a child of my own potentially unattainable. We talked this situation over and he became uneasy. He was (and still is) protective of his little girls and we were already bonding. They welcomed me into their home with warmth and love which made the prospect of me potentially deciding at some point in the future to walk away, should my desire to have a child of my own become more important to me, all the more scary. It was tough, but the situation created a distance between us.

This is where fate played a hand. Aside from polite text messages, we hadn't seen each other for a few days when outside my house, I was moving some boxes and tripped and fell awkwardly in a heap on the floor. My ankle instantly swelled, and I couldn't move. So, who did I reach out to? Instinctively, I called your dad (spoiler alert) – I needed help, I couldn't move! It felt like exactly the right thing to do. He was there in minutes, with two wide-eyed girls in the back of the car, ready to nurse me back to strength. Lifting me into the back of the car, your dad was calm and kind, whilst nurse Charlotte fed me medicine, in the form of minstrels, and nurse Sophie checked my wound.

Plenty of rest later, your dad and I were stronger than ever, but the awkward conversation of babies hadn't been re-addressed. A couple of weeks passed when we were in a shopping centre and happened to walk through the baby clothes department. Hearing my name called I turned to see your dad holding a pair of baby boots, wearing a massive grin – he had changed his mind!

If I had not fallen, your dad and I may never have fully reconciled. Yes, it was painful, both emotionally and physically but, holding onto my now deep-rooted belief that we are exactly where we are meant to be, I can see now that I was moving in a direction that was wrong for me. In falling, I had to stop moving that way and rest up. Because I fell, the direction I was heading in pivoted, and my path corrected.

Four house moves, a wedding, numerous job changes and a mortgage later, we were ready to add to our family. We would absolutely have had a baby sooner but, there were already four of us and there was never enough room, nor enough money to agree it was the right time. Now I know, a baby at any other time would not have been *you* and for that, I am eternally grateful we waited. Because of who you are, I can see that deciding to have you when we did was exactly the right time.

Still buzzing with the mix of joy and nerves of a positive pregnancy test, the words from the voice on the other end of the phone nearly swiped my legs from under me. It was the hospital "Mrs. Myers, you need to come in as soon as possible." I was eight-weeks pregnant, and the bloods taken at my doctors' surgery the day before had raised the alarm.

Working over two hours from the hospital, I wouldn't make it there that day, so I endured a sleepless night, knowing I had to rush to the maternity ward in the morning. Here we met Rose, our specialist nurse, who explained that blood I had received from an earlier transfusion must have been contaminated. My body's reaction to this foreign intruder was to produce antibodies to fight it. The reality is, this intruder was no threat, I didn't even know of its existence until this very moment, sitting here shaking in the hospital room, hoping with all of my being that this was not bad news for my baby.

This antibody, Anti-K (produced to defend against Kell, the presence of which was in the transfusion I received) was in fact only a threat to you if you developed with your dad's blood line. Mine would not be seen as a danger and would not awaken this sleeping army.

We were monitored very closely, I may as well have moved into the hospital, with all the blood tests and extra scans. I felt I never left, but the hospital had our backs and I got to see you on the tiny monitor more than most mums-to-be and every result was one closer to meeting you in real life.

You brought me joy from the moment I knew you were there, my giggles at your incessant hiccups would interrupt very important work meetings daily! You would salsa around my belly, whenever the Strictly Come Dancing theme tune would play; putting it on repeat, your dad and sisters would gather around my bump to feel and watch your best moves in action.

Whilst there was much joy and excitement, behind my smile I was still back on high alert, were these misplaced protectors, silently charging their battalion to throw us off course? The specialists were prepared to deliver you at 28-weeks, if the antibodies were engaged, you would be safer in an incubator than growing in me – my body could be your worst enemy.

Despite the risk, you made it to full-term, and a week more, only starting your descent, when your dad and I had completed a pub crawl of Surrey's finest (I was on the orange juice of course). The labour was long, 40 hours in total so given the drawing out, you were checked regularly for signs of distress. All proving well, the midwife even commented on how calm you were. She said:"Baby just calmly does as they are told". Everyone was keen for a natural delivery, so we waited and waited until finally you decided to make your appearance.

I can't tell you if it is instinct or it is from what we have seen on TV but parents waiting for the arrival of their new blood are programmed to hear a piercing cry, even a screech when they meet the bright lights and clatter of the delivery room. When you arrived, there was nothing, not a peep, silence. I was woozy but I still panicked, and I could see the look on your dad's face and it didn't reassure me.

You were taken out of the room for what felt like hours, when you returned, you were handed straight to your dad with a cheerful introductory: "He just doesn't cry" from the midwife. I can corroborate that from (almost) that moment forward you have been the calmest, kindest, most delightful boy I could ever have wished for.

How can love be wrong?

I have been told, by many people, especially in the early years of your life, that I will "ruin" you. I have been very open and vocal about how special you are. I showered you with love from the minute I knew I was carrying you and, no doubt, still do. In fact, it took vast inner strength not to get a tattoo of your face on my arm and produce a line of Sebastian merch. I'll have to hope that writing a book for you, about you and dedicated to you proves I kept my love low key!

I can very safely say that without your dad's parental experience and teaching background, being sure to set boundaries early on and to be clear on discipline, we would probably be in a whole heap of trouble – you could quite possibly be running rings around me!

As far as "ruining" you though, I struggle to justify in my mind why being sure that you know how loved you are is wrong? It may well come back to bite me in the future, or worse, bite you. If 'they' were right all along and there is some connection with being loved as a child and delusions of grandeur in later years then I am sorry but, even then remember, I did what I thought was right at the time and you are not broken!

We are exactly where we are meant to be

The initial part of our history is never to be misunderstood for you not being part of either of our plans. At that moment in time, we had no plans, we were a new couple and had many challenges of our own, as a duo and as a new 'blended family'. I may well have gone on to start a different family but, *you* would not be *you* if I had not fallen and hurt my foot. You are exactly you because of this history and are indeed perfect because of it too. Whilst my ankle was painful and resting to heal was frustrating, my direction was meant to change. I didn't know it at the time, and I was not at this level of understanding, it is only with this new outlook that I can see the significance of this event.

It's not just through path-changing events that this is demonstrated, I prove this theory every day. Before I believed it, if somebody would have said to me that my path is already decided and that worrying about the future or regretting the past is pointless, life plays out exactly as it is meant to, I would have visions of hippies and unicorns – I would have questioned the message givers state-of-mind. But, over time I ran tests, starting small and expanding the scale of the outcome the more confident I became.

Initially, I would giggle when the landing light being left on meant traipsing back upstairs, reminding me that my handbag was still on the bed. Had I not needed to turn the light off, I would have left the house without my phone, purse etc.

Another example was my disappointment to have been let down over and over again by a series of builders. Not showing up, never sending quotes, not answering calls. We were wanting to convert a garage, initially for space for your sisters to use as a crash pad when visiting from their various universities but more recently, since Covid-19 meant I fully worked from home, I wanted a proper space to work from. I managed in our dark and air free basement for so long, but I needed something more suitable.

What I now know is we were *not* ready; I am thankful to all of those who did not respond. We needed more time to prepare, to cement our ideas and when we did, a builder was there, right in front of us working at a house a few doors up. Without the delay, we could have got into a mess including not being financially ready.

Now, I marvel daily at how this understanding shows itself to me, and the marvel helps me to stay in the present. I have built my own faith that I am exactly where I am meant to be. Every event, positive or not, happens for a reason. The reason could present itself to me immediately, like the handbag on the bed. It could take years, like the fall when I was carrying boxes or, I may never know but, simply believing that wasting energy seeking answers, carrying the weight of the past or fearing future outcomes is taking valuable energy from my experience.

This faith is an instant calmer. Should I feel myself second guessing or over-thinking a situation, a brief and silent reminder to myself that 'what is meant to be will be' melts any unease away right there and then. It is like the distraction of my discomfort evaporates, seconds after it innocently arrives, placing me neatly back in the peace of just simply *being*.

In fact, on the topic of seeking answers, having this faith also means no longer replaying conversations, situations or holding on to negative emotions about other people's actions. As Michael Neill writes: **"Our thoughts are the camera, our eyes are the lens. Put them together and the picture we see is reality."**

My extension of this is that life is full of ups and downs, cheer and sorrow. If your life is a film, you are the director. It is entirely your choice where you point the camera. Focusing your thinking on moments that brought fear, pain or ill feeling will deliver you a movie of horror, sadness and anger. Transversally, you can decide to point your camera at the joy, wonder and amusement in your life. This is not to say pain does not exist but, within which genre do you choose to live your life?"

We get what we need when we need it

This level of understanding has proven to me that we get what we need when we need it. This may or may not refer to what we want materialistically (I will let you decide how to make the differentiation) – in fact, if what you think you need does not appear, I challenge you to wonder, did I really need that?

This, for me, applies to support, belongings, essentials, money, opportunities, rest, lessons, and challenges. In fact, it applies to all levels and layers of my experience. You can choose to focus on what you don't have or to be happy with what you do.

I cannot, though, reason this approach to severe illness, grief, or war. But that is because I have not experienced it. I will not say I have lived a sheltered life, it certainly has not been, but I am lucky that I have not, well not really, had to suffer these extremes.

I can tell you though that, in considering how I will cope when inevitably faced with one or another, I know I will be ok. The impact that could have previously rocked every part of my world from these events, what I call my blast radius, is tight.

Now my strength comes from my core, not from what I perceive others think of me, others behaviour towards me or what is going on around me. I still feel emotion, I am not a robot, I get sad when sadness is due, I feel frustration and despair and surprise and that is absolutely ok, but my mind is overall peaceful, and my inner strength no longer shatters on impact.

Setting your blast radius

Someone I know gets, in my opinion, too close to other vehicles. I was taught by my driving instructor two things; TNT and only a fool breaks the five second rule. TNT, not the explosive, stands for tyres n' tarmac - when you come to a stop behind another vehicle, always stop far enough to be able to see the point that the back tyres of the vehicle in front are touching the tarmac.

The science behind this is that if the car behind you slams into your boot, you still have space to shunt forward before you bump into the next vehicle. Your space could mean the difference between a bumper bump and a multi-vehicle pile-up. The other space saver is if the car in front of you rolls back, you have time to warn them with your horn before they bump your front end.

The five second rule, refers to the space you should leave between you and the car in front when travelling at speed. Pick a stationary point in front of you, like a lamp post or bridge. When the rear bumper of the car in front passes this point, count in seconds until you reach the same point, any less than five full seconds and you are too close, hang back to create more space.

In both of these scenarios, not leaving enough space puts you (and everyone in your vehicle) at risk. More than this, it puts anyone else close to you at risk too.

Now add to the mix how you react when others get too close or cut you up. Pity the car that swerves ahead of this too close driver or jumps the queue – they proceed to drive right up close and tail the driver until their anger has passed. This can happen in a slow-moving queue or it can even happen in the fast lane of the motorway. Rage takes over and introduced risk is ignored, it is more important to this driver to show who is boss than safety. What also gets ignored is that they are compounding the risk that they were already too close in the first place.

I have so many questions here;

Why not just leave a little more space, just a bit can make a big difference?

Why do you feel the need to show the other drivers you are frustrated by ignoring your own risk and getting even closer, you don't know them and will never see them again in your life – they are not important!?

But then I also consider this scenario in our everyday lives.

Why do we allow other people's behaviour to impact our own in a way that puts our valuable wellbeing at risk? Can you see how this happens in all areas of our lives? And how little sense it makes when you realise that you can control your behaviour, not that of those around you and that the most important thing you can do is protect yourself.

This field of protection is what I call setting your blast radius. Let's consider that an explosion were to happen, a drama in your friendship circle, a problem in your family, an issue at work. Or on a bigger scale in newsworthy politics, an alarming headline, or a shocking world event – your blast radius is how far into your core you allow the tremors of that explosion, or blast, to be felt.

I can absolutely promise you, how far the blast affects you is 100 percent your decision to make. The blast can be small enough that you just stand tall, dust yourself down and reclaim your power.

There are many scenarios whereby you cannot control what happens to you. In every scenario, you cannot control other people's actions but what you do 100 percent have control over however, is how you react. Choose to drive too close to prove you are frustrated or allow those that are getting too close to you the space they need to get on with their own choices whilst you do your utmost to protect your radius.

You have nothing to prove to anyone you don't even know. You in fact, don't have anything to prove to anyone

you do know.

Slow down, hang back, observe without reaction.

You have already demonstrated to me your ability to do this. When you were small and playing in a group, in instances of conflict between people around you like a bickering brother and sister, I would beam at how you instinctively walked away.

Rather than get involved or dragged into the drama, you removed yourself from the situation without fuss or panic and just moved on to something else, even if it meant playing alone.

In most situations, not getting involved is often simplest and the best option for protecting your calm. Drama attracts drama so keeping out of the way altogether has the opposite impact. I am not suggesting however in situations where a person is being hurt or singled out you should turn away, here trust your wisdom to guide your action. However old you are or how senior your position, usually sharing what you have seen with a person of authority is the best approach.

Peace over judgement

I have just shared with you my judgement of this person's driving - everybody judges, it's natural, the small, nagging voice in your head alerts you to a person's actions, appearance, or words. But why? What is right for one may be the opposite for another. Our values all differ, as do our priorities. Comparing our own approach to that of another is pointless, we are not the same. And isn't that great!

With a little inner-training, not giving power to that voice in the first place, I hope that you realise that judgement is little more than untrustworthy mind chatter, even that of other people's minds.

By realising that other people's opinions of you are not what sets your value, and approaching your life for your own outcome, not what other people may think of you, judgement will be less and less in focus.

I used to desperately run around tidying the house if I knew somebody could be popping by. But now, I just open the door (ok, so I hide the washing and load the dishwasher!) and am proud that how they judge my clutter is absolutely none of my business, that is up to them and how loud their inner voice is. If it is a problem for them, that says more about them than about me.

The same goes for my hair – although I try to make the best of it, my hair just does its own thing anyway!

I wish for you to embrace your own choices without fear of judgement.

Wear what you want to wear and let others do the same. Somebody looks different, that's cool.

Somebody has a different view to you, no worries.

Choosing a different direction, I hope it is peaceful and I send hope for enjoyment and best wishes.

3 A life of ADVENTURE

Coach and trainer David Key shared a story of when his stepfather's deteriorating health consumed his mother's sparkle. He was on his deathbed and her worry for him was all she could focus on. David re-framed this situation for her, did she want to spend these last few days and weeks distracted by an inevitable event in the future of which nothing she does has any consequence OR, did she want to spend what time was left laughing and bringing joy to their final moments together.

This struck a chord with me, whilst I am not in this situation, nobody is getting any younger. We can choose to live our lives distracted by topics or events we have no control over or as if every day is a gift.

Growing up, I was a free spirit, Granny called me a butterfly, fluttering from petal to petal, adventure to adventure. I took a job as a nanny in Italy, straight from completing my GCSE's, returning to take a job with an electronics company where a basic understanding of the Italian language was a requirement. On weekends, I would visit friends all over the country, dancing, singing, living it up as a carefree teenager would.

Leaving school as early as I did, university was not an option. Moving to Birmingham for work, aged 17, was my version of the rite of passage students undertake, it was fun. But, sadly, it was short-lived as my life took a totally different turn, when I had a car accident. This resulted in four inches of bone in both of my femurs shattering, my collar bone breaking, my shoulder dislocating, a hernia and nerve damage in my shin, fragments of car parts sticking out from my neck, eyelid and hand as well as many cuts and bruises.

Surgery to fit bi-lateral titanium femoral implants, which remain in place to this day, plus blood transfusions led to an extended stay in hospital. Following this, I had to learn to walk again, finally walking unaided 18 months later. But, I sure did have fun in my wheelchair, still getting out and about, being carried around nightclubs by burly bouncers and befriending my own personal taxi driver who was kind and made sure I was safe and always got home.

JR, my personal cabby picked me up one weekend from a festival in the middle of a boggy field in south Oxfordshire. My wheels were 2-3 inches thick with mud but he still pushed me into the back of his black cab, making a two am stop at a jet-wash, hosing the mud off to protect my parent's carpet. He joined us at parties too, using his cab as the stereo system, taking requests, and making everybody laugh with his crazy stories.

People you are meant to meet

One evening, I went out to a bar with friends in my wheelchair of course, my go -faster stripes and pom poms were in place. My friends were chatting away to people we had met, probably having a dance but I needed the loo! Struggling to get myself there, I was unsteady on my wheels when a lady crouched down to my level.

"I don't want to offend you; I am not sure whether to offer, but, do you need some help?"

"Yes!" I said, "I just need to get to the bathroom and then I need another drink." Back at the bar, we chatted and she introduced herself as a producer of a BBC radio station. She asked me if I would be interviewed about; how to approach offers of help to people with disabilities without causing offence?

My quick response was: "Why not?" I've never spoken on the radio before but, apart from some volunteering with the British Red Cross, I wasn't working, as I was focusing on intensive rehabilitation.

Within weeks, I was offered a regular spot, making local announcements and introducing guests as well as being trained as a broadcast assistant, being in control of the sliders and fielding incoming callers on the evening request show. This role grew even further and I was taken on as a local sports broadcaster, yes, your very own mum, reporting on live football games every weekend.

I didn't have a clue about the rules of football so I would skip the press box, opting to sit in the crowd, listening to their chatter to repeat on air. I also dragged Granny along, being great with words, she helped me make my report sound credible.

Somebody at the BBC came up with a nickname for me, I was: *"Danie Vee, the lady with the latest."* At one point, I even had my own jingle, let me know if you want to hear it…!

For many reasons, money being one of them, I moved on from the 'Beeb'. I was out of the wheelchair and gradually progressed from walking with a frame to just using sticks and finally I was walking with just one stick. Although I had a blast and learned so much, I didn't see a future for me there.

I sometimes wonder, without regret, what would've happened if I stayed? Would I be on screen now reporting on Premiership games, oh how proud you would be of me, I have never known a bigger football fan than you - Up the Villa!

Just say "Yes."

I didn't set out to be on the radio, but I said: "Yes", and I've done the same for pretty much all the opportunities that have presented themselves to me. Whilst I do of course wonder what on earth I will be getting myself into and if I even have the skills, I decide to not let that wondering get in the way of just going for it. Remember, being brave is feeling scared but doing it anyway.

I wish for you to have a sense of adventure like mine, for you to not let doubt get in the way of saying yes to what comes your way. We all get doubt, it is natural but action beats fear and once you have done something a few times, it isn't scary anymore.

In the early days of this journey, I was introduced to the stretch zone; whilst your comfort zone is just that, comfortable, your stretch zone, the area within which you grow, can feel uncomfortable...stretchy! Once you repeat this action and it becomes easier, your comfort zone expands to meet you here, you grow with it and the stretchiness becomes comfort once again.

High flying

The adventures continued throughout my life, personal and career wise. From being forcibly removed from a stage, escorted through Jeddah by armed guards to honeymooning in Las Vegas. Partying on the 70th floor of the Swiss Hotel in Singapore to dining as a family at the Shard for your sister's 21st.

When you were very small, your dad studied for his masters

degree. It meant weekends spent at a laptop for him and as a way of supporting that, I planned for us to be out of the way as much as we could, we can be quite distracting!

I started taking you to soft play centres and for picnics in the park but always having an appetite for adventure, I switched it up a bit. When you were two I took you to Nice, your sisters tagged along and we journeyed along the French riviera coast by train to Monaco. You gazed open jawed at the crystal sea and mega yachts; I don't think you quite believed what was in front of your eyes.

Twice we took week's away in Tenerife and even ventured to '*Wonderful Wonderful Copenhagen,*' for a weekend – all to help your dad with his studies of course, how selfless of us!

The trips we took were not extravagant, I would book cheap flights and use previously collected hotel points for our accommodation. Often our trips would cost less than a train ticket to London, but wow did we have some fun! You are one special travel buddy.

Sadly, Covid-19 stopped our fun little trips but, I wish for you, when you can, to always have an adventure to daydream about. Even just time away from your normal routine, apparently a change is as good as a rest.

What do you think?

When I was at my lowest point of the downward spiral that triggered my transformation, I couldn't even look forward to holidays. As well as my unhealthy lifestyle and lack of quality sleep, negative thinking was feeding my low state. Within this low state, not much was exciting, including the poor decisions I was making.

As you know, I have gone on to train as a coach. David Key's Ultimate Coach Programme totally restructured how I see the world and introduced me to some wonderful like-minded people*.

The approach this programme is based on is called the Three Principles (3Ps), first introduced by Sydney Banks. This understanding and my subsequent learning prompted me to set up my coaching practice, Executive Leap. Here I focus on helping people struggling with stress at work and executive burn-out (takes one to know one).

Through the 3Ps, I have discovered so much about how we shape our own experience, simply through the thoughts we give power too.

I have learned how powerful our thoughts are. I have learned how, although we cannot so much as control our thoughts, we can control how we engage with them. I have also learned that, like training any other part of our body or brain, with practice, we can become skilled at 'managing' how we respond to our thinking.

Before this realisation, I had no understanding of thought, of thinking and of how much a part it plays in how we live our lives. I believed that thoughts happened to me, were all true and that they defined me. I believed in labels and that one person can be an over-thinker and that they could allow that to shape the rest of their lives, whilst the next person could be a negative thinker and in the same way, that misunderstanding could brand them that way forever with no escape.

But now I know better.

Try this; next time you have an itch, without movement imagine that it is being scratched. With all of your power, think to yourself that your itch has fingernails pressing back and forth for a few seconds. It has gone, right?! It may initially return but keep imagining and with practice, over time, you will learn this inner control. Give it a go!

Next try this; when you forget what you were about to say, instead of racking around your mind desperately trying to summon the words, empty it. Divert your thinking from the forgotten topic and you will see that it will appear. If clearing your mind is not yet natural, think of something totally separate to what you are currently considering. Recall a holiday or a memory that prompts a smile – I am confident that your forgotten thought returns simply.

You see, I have begun to understand thinking and that I can present a level of authority over it, I see my mind as a slightly separate part of me. I envision 'thinking' as a toddler vying for my attention, prepared to fib or create drama so as not to be ignored. Equally, a toddler can love unconditionally and complement without judgement. A toddler learns boundaries by testing them first so once you realise not everything you think is there to serve you, be clear on the thoughts you are prepared to be led by.

I have also recognised that a toddler's default position is joy. They are more drawn to love and would rather be friends than not friends. Responsibility does not inhibit joy in a child. Give them a job or a toy to look after and the job becomes a focus, it becomes what is most 'important' in that moment and not a burden. They feel innately secure which leads to a state of responsiveness, a positive 'can do' mindset that is not about whether they know what they are doing.

A child's initial reaction is not one of insecurity. Feeling insecure does not tell you about you, it tells you about what you think about yourself and a child's inner critic has not yet been given the power of authority.

Now, my emotional IQ comes from understanding my triggers and knowing not to take my thinking too seriously. I question the outcome I actually want, what result serves me and does my inner toddler's focus support this? If not, I know what to do…

Did you know, every human being has between 60,000 and 90,000 thoughts every single day? Imagine an iceberg, the tip above the water represents the thoughts we give power to, beneath the surface are those thoughts that we can keep within our subconscious, not needed for now. Thoughts that we do not need and will not need in the future, can be left to float away on the waves of an endless sea.

It's like when you drive a car, I don't know if you do yet, but, go with me on this one…. When you learn to drive, all the information you are taking in and need to get through your lesson stays at the tip of the iceberg, it's new and not yet committed to your intellect, your inner wisdom if you like, which sits in the base of the iceberg. The more you drive, the less you need these instructions in the tip. They can go beneath the surface to be called upon by your consciousness when you need them. Get to a roundabout, get the knowledge on how to navigate it, at this moment you don't need to know how to parallel park.

By being selective about what you allow to stay in the tip of your iceberg, will shape your experience. By focusing on the things that are going wrong, feeding the negative state can act as a magnet for negative behaviour – for me, low mood thinking equals a low mood which equals low mood behaviour. I know that I have the tendency to feed a negative state with bad food and low mood decisions, feeling sorry for myself and blaming others. Setting a positive purpose, like the toddler with an 'important' job, and filling my iceberg tip with alternatives, can instantly change my mood and therefore my behaviour. A purposeful,

positive iceberg tip leads to purposeful, positive behaviour.

A revelation to me was learning that good and bad thoughts cannot be in your mind at the same time. Boom! Mastery! It sounds too simple but choosing to replace that negativity with something that turns a frown upside down changes me in that very instant.

Baby steps

For some people, this knowledge is enough to elevate their experience – they can take this and shape it to many areas of current discomfort and be on their happy, merry forever to be joyful way.

For most though, it takes some testing of the water to believe that you have control over your own thinking and that this power can change the whole world within and around you.

I started with small changes. My first step on this mind changing ladder was distraction. I set about building up happy topics to focus on when negativity overwhelmed me.

I began with creating a photo album on my phone full of photos, mainly of you, that made me smile. Then, a playlist that made me want to dance or sing at the top of my lungs, even if I got the words wrong. Creating playlists led to investigating new music, artists I had never heard of would blast my ears for hours, successfully drowning out any overthinking.

Soon, I opened up to considering adventures again, researching destinations and planning trips was another worthy distraction. I began to realise that this simplicity is indeed a reality. A simple smile to replace a frown can be all it takes.

Whatever lowered my brow initially will still be there when I have scrolled all the pictures or sang all the songs but my clearer mind, without all the low mood fog will be able to process it better, with a better ultimate outcome and calmer resulting behaviour. The more practice I got, the easier this became and now I no longer needed the replacement in my berg tip, I can in fact almost empty the tip completely and be at peace within the space between my thoughts.

I wish for you to know that you can fill your "iceberg tip" with thoughts that lift your mood. You are 100 percent in control of the thoughts you give power too, and when one pops in that could do the opposite, replace it or better still, let it pass on by like a cloud. It may be simple to master, or it may take some practice, but it really is possible, I am proof.

I heard once in passing that if children are getting agitated to either take them outside or put them in water so if you are still looking for distraction, taking a shower or a walk is the adult equivalent.

I used to try to guide you this way when you were small, "think of something different" I would say, or "let's just think of nothing together" but initially it didn't make sense to you. You would tell me that if somebody tells you what to think of, it didn't work, in fact it could somehow make it worse. That makes sense to me, and I can see that it is the same for many just learning of this approach. Imagine I asked you NOT to think of a green triangle? Yep, there it is!

Knowing that there was a way to guide you that I hadn't yet thought of, I didn't give up and one night it came to me. Like me you love to sing and if a song was a perfect starter step for me, why not you?

Your favourite song of that time was 'I'm Still Standing,' by

Elton John, it was from a movie you loved and you sang it over and over. Whatever the song, you would wake up singing, sing in the car, the bath in the toilet and in bed at night. So why not when your thoughts are overwhelming or lowering your mood?

You tried it, thinking of the words of your favourite song in your head, rhythmically reciting them to your own beat. The grin spread across your face – it was working. At the time of writing this book, I hope that with practice, after a while you don't need me to remind you of this tool, you do it instinctively.

Quality over quantity

Once you have proven, through replacement or distraction, that it is possible to have power over your own experience, the next step up the ladder of consciousness is letting poor thoughts go altogether.

Please know that I am not here encouraging you to push all negative thoughts into the iceberg below the surface, this approach is not about feeling or thought suppression. It's about deciding to only entertain thinking that serves you, understanding the difference between good and bad quality thoughts.

Again, some may pick this up straight away, for others it may take practice. Once mastered though it can mean the difference between dragging your heels along with head hung low and skipping with knees high and arms swishing for no apparent reason, just because you decide to be happy.

Some may think I live with my head in the clouds, avoiding reality with the potential of letting people walk all over me but I can absolutely promise you that is not the case. What I do is decide to let in what is necessary and field what is not, based on how I decide to live my life.

This way of living gives me more clarity on what is important, more time for what I enjoy and makes me assertive in setting my personal boundaries. It makes me more efficient, I don't have to spend my days skipping through a meadow to feel free, I can find nuggets of peace and bliss within the dullest of tasks.

It's useful to recognise that some thoughts do serve as warnings, they may not feel great but they are still good quality – your instinct's reaction to a situation. Trusting that instinct, acting upon that thought without allowing it to affect your mood is recognising its quality in parallel to maintaining quality boundaries, not spiraling into a low mood.

We do all still feel low moods though and decision making in a low mood can result in low mood decisions. My recommendation for you is to hold off on making decisions until this mood has passed, which it will. Better still, don't bother making decisions anymore at all. If the answer is clear, showing itself to you with clarity, it is not really a decision, it is an action to take. If it's not clear, you are not ready to take the action. When you have all the information you need, that clarity will be instinctive – it will come from your wisdom. Given that you are exactly where you are meant to be, right at that moment, all you need to do is wait for the clarity, not force the answer.

Always seeking a higher solution though, I have recently added this gem to my armory. In a low mood, hunt to help. The act of helping others, donating time, belongings or money re-fills the iceberg with powerfully good intention. An inner glow that zaps any uninvited poor-quality thoughts.

The Ultimate Coach programme is full to bursting with kindhearted people helpers. If ever you bump into any of my fellow coaches, take a moment to listen to their wisdom, you won't regret it!

A lot of respect from me to Linda, Dave, Jon, Jimmy, Dawn, Tracey, Chris,

Frederica, Wanda, Mark, Simon, Ed, Kate, Kevin and the rest of the UCP band of warm souls.

4 A life of PURPOSE

I was commuting for more than two hours each way to work and it consumed me. This was before I understood thought and I couldn't shake a constant feeling of dread. I loved my job, the people, my achievements, and the work I did was important, but I couldn't lift myself out of the low mood that having to travel so far sunk me into.

My head was heavy with all of my negative thinking, overflowing with no room left for anything that could possibly bring me joy. Often, I had to leave for work before you woke and when I returned, you were asleep. I would sit on your bedroom floor crying that how much I missed you, physically hurt.

A business I had launched wasn't working out, I carried the pressure of my job around with me and there were parts of my life within which I felt taken advantage of. I was also under the misconception that as long as I was doing everything I could to make sure everyone else around me was 'ok', I was doing a good job.

This overflow spiraled into my physical health, not surprising as I was feeding this low feeling with a dangerous cocktail of sugary, processed foods, coffee, sweeteners, and alcohol. I wasn't sleeping, overplaying conversations in my mind and doubting my actions of the previous day.

My mind wasn't just busy, it was over-run. I now know I was ignoring the 'red flag' warning signs. Low moods, paranoia that I was doing a bad job, due to being overwhelmed with toxic thinking. Instead of recognising I was being warned, I was trying to block them out with my poor lifestyle choices. So, the alarm bells had to ring louder, I started having panic attacks.

Extreme claustrophobia set in, crowded places caused me to panic, blood rushing to my head, heart pounding, sweats, desperation to escape. I would have an attack on a busy train, a tube and once I even had an attack when the zip on my coat got stuck. People around me would tell me to breathe and this would anger me more. But I *still* didn't listen to the warning.

I developed an allergy to what I now know to be fragrance. It took years to finally get to the answer, all the while, my skin flaring up in patches of burning red blisters on my neck and head, I felt like flaming hot lava was pouring down my forehead. The inflammation caused my hair to fall out in massive clumps.

Losing my hair was the final 'red flag' signal I needed. I had to listen to my body, I couldn't ignore it; I was too afraid of losing it all. This fear was real and overwhelming, like an elastic band pinging…

I went snap.

I knew I had to do something about this and in my quest to find out what my skin was reacting with I began working with a coach. Anna changed my life. One of the first things she said to me was: "You've got to put on your own life jacket first." To be able to truly be there for anyone else; your family, people that rely on you at work, your community, you have to look after yourself first. If you are already sinking, you have no chance of looking after them'.

It was a game-changer. Who was I kidding to think I could be a good mum, step-mum, wife, leader, mentor when inside I was a mess? Anna challenged me to look at things differently, to reframe my situation. In my heart, I knew I needed to work closer to home but at a time when working outside of London usually meant a huge drop in income, I had to find a way to have it all.

In reframing my situation, Anna gifted me four hours a day of study time, precious time I could devote completely to fueling my plan to take you to school and pick you up as often as I possibly could. My commute, the part of my life I hated the most, became my route back up and out of this negative spiral.

I crammed in as much learning as I could, and this became my purpose. I would look forward to my commute, (yes, a first) I switched to brain food starting my day with a nuclear green smoothie – packed with 7, 8, 9 of my five-a-day. The menial tasks that would usually frustrate me at work became insignificant, just a necessary action to take in my journey to commute freedom. I attached no emotion to the task, it just was, not good or bad.

Over the months, things got better and better, I had more energy and rather than feeling like a victim, I was able to have conversations to reset expectations where I felt advantage was being taken. In finally looking after myself, I had an inner strength to set boundaries that I hadn't considered before.

The amazing thing is this reset wasn't difficult. I had stories in my head that being honest and open about where I was at and what I needed from people would be awful. That I would lose my job or argue with friends but, the only thing that changed was the spring in my step.

I also realised that if those conversations had been difficult, I would still be ok. That one conversation is not the complete definition of me and if it did not go as I hoped, we could either keep talking and work it out or I could decide that this situation was not in my best interests.

As it so happened, this was the case with my job. There was an element of my responsibilities that was genuinely impossible. With my new clarity I could see that this was not just me seeing everything through fog coated glasses, it was too much for anyone so, with the company I worked for sticking to their guns on this point, I moved on.

Whilst my new role was still a commute away, I didn't dread the journey anymore, I continued to learn and progressed into different areas. I was not afraid to invest in myself either. Many adults feel guilty for spending their money on their own development. We happily invest in music and dance lessons for our children, so why is it wrong for us to invest in something similar for ourselves? For joy or for knowledge, I gained many qualifications and learned for interest, not just monetary or status gain. I found joy in this purpose and often wished for broken down trains and closed lines. Not because I didn't want to come home, never think that, but because my level of consciousness had shifted.

I am not living in the weeds anymore, I don't get stuck on small inconveniences, I take hurdles in my stride, after all, I am exactly where I am meant to be right at this very moment and that hurdle is mine for the jumping. I may not know where I am going but each day is another opportunity to take one more step in the right direction.

I also proved the importance of good sleep. Frequently running a car close to empty, seeps the dregs from the bottom of the tank into the engine, compounding over time, this clogs up the pipes, slowing the car and impacting performance. Eventually, the car will bellow smoke, its output compromised.

Sleep is of course crucial for resetting your energy levels which improves focus and ultimate output. Sayings like 'things will be better after a good night's sleep' ring true. Rather than heading to the pub after a bad day or dwelling on a tough meeting, an early night can have a far better outcome. Save the pub for social occasions, not as a tool to drown out a busy mind.

In times when sleep isn't your friend, have a go at this; fill your iceberg with sweeping motions and calming actions like choreographing a synchronised swimming routine or a trampolining sequence. Try conducting an orchestra or snowboarding down an intricate course in slow motion. With each movement, in your head only, gracefully extend your required limb, paying attention to the deep breathing required to deliver on this task you are focusing fully on creating. Once the sequence is complete, relax that limb, concentrating on laying it in the perfect position to rest, untensing it with each long, drawn out breath – this works for me!

Sender to the rescue

Living through the Covid-19 pandemic was unusual. It was tough for many and for them I understand and have sympathy but, I personally didn't struggle. Yes of course, there were bad days but the changes to our lives delivered me all I was longing for at that time.

Only two months into the first Covid-19 lockdown, the company I contracted most of my hours to at that time closed their office, permanently. I still worked for them but only from home and at the point of writing this, it has not changed.

Even though a further two years later, in this country we

opened back up again, there was no intention of ever opening another physical office. Even though my commute dread had dispersed, I still saddened at being so far away from you – well from this moment I walked you to school every day, collected you and read your bedtime story far more than I ever did before Covid-19 made an appearance.

That said, I know there were struggles. During one of the many lockdowns, I was aware that you and many children around your age started displaying signs of anxiety.

Your dad and I as well as your sisters tried to help you in the obvious ways; being supportive and encouraging you to focus on things you enjoy but who am I to help...I am just mum, right?

The timing coincided with a challenge set by a fellow coach Jo – to publish a book in 6 months. In thinking up different ways to get my words of advice across, I wondered whether I could blend this writing challenge with drafting in your imaginary friend Sender. So, with your fifth birthday in three months, I targeted the date to present you with a personal gift, a book about winners, losers, and fun – publishing may or may not have come later.

I started writing and the words kept flowing and by the big day, I had a book, bound and printed at our local print shop, wrapped and ready to present to you as a big surprise.

You were open-mouthed; your first delighted words were: "Can we put this in shops so other children can read it?" Surprised by how much I enjoyed the whole process I replied: "Why not - we have nothing to lose!" and here the **Sender Feels Better** series was born – a simple ditty I wrote for your birthday became a purpose of wider contribution for me, a welcomed focus through Covid-19 uncertainty.

Written from the heart, the 'moral' within each story is based on the techniques I learned when training to coach. I weaved in tools and approaches to re-frame situations and manage uncomfortable emotions. The stories are intended to be layered; engaging character journeys, each with an underlying message of positive mental health.

The inspiration I took for the characters in the main friendship circle comes from the imaginary friends that have been a part of my family for years. The most recent being the main character Sender, your imaginary friend, who has joined us on holidays and for dinner at our table since you were about two. We have even celebrated Sender's birthday…regularly…I am sure he manages to have more birthdays than Queen Elizabeth II, it could be because we have cake?

Sender's friends Goo and Eny, my older brother's imaginary friends when he was small. They too shared family holidays, played in our garden and fell asleep with us at bedtime between the years of about 1978 and 1983.

Overall, the series is aimed at 4–7-year-old children's curious imaginations, each story touching upon different triggers from boredom to anger, over-competitiveness to loneliness.

Sender's little soldiers

You were struggling to get to sleep at night. There was so much talk of illness around, I was not surprised that this seeped its way to you. You would cry, worrying whether you would wake up in the morning. 'What will happen to me in the night?' you would sob. You would imagine blood too, 'am I bleeding?' being a regular question. To calm your over-active mind at bedtime, I wrote one of the Sender books focused around how sleep is a master of healing.

The story elaborates on a tactic my mum would tell me when I was young. When Sender hurts his hand, his friend Eny helps him discover what he needs to do to feel better. This book tells the story of Sender's friend Eny encouraging him to get some rest after he injured his hand in a fall. Feeling a bit bruised and sorry for himself, Sender learns that his body's little soldiers can only get to work to fix him back up when he is fast asleep.

Even after a few good night's sleep, Sender is left with a scar on his hand. In my book, I sow the seed that even though the mark may not fade, it does not stop Sender from getting up and having more fun with his friends.

We all have scars, things don't always go well. I can tell you first hand, scars – not just physical ones, are part of the journey, not the end of it.

Bed-time blues

Your dad has always been very good at introducing and keeping to routines for you. We always read you a bedtime story before you would go to sleep. You also listened to classical piano music in your room at bedtime, (very sophisticated indeed).

When your Covid-19 struggles appeared at bedtime though, after each story, I would recite a series of phrases that I hoped would help you calm for the night, they went like this;

- o ***I am ready to fall asleep**
- o ***I am safe**
- o ***I am perfect exactly as I am**
- o ***I love my family very much**
- o ***My family love me very much**
- o ***I will put my mind to what will help me sleep**

A few days after we started this routine, you asked to introduce some new words to the list and continued to recite:

- o ***A great attitude becomes a great day**
- o ***Which becomes a great week**
- o ***Which becomes a great month**
- o ***Which becomes a great year**
- o ***Which becomes a great life**

You got this from school, and it stuck with us both, it's actually so true. For me, the attitude in question is an attitude of purpose. Once you have got into the habit of setting a purpose each day, it will become second nature to always live a life of purpose. I am not, at this stage, talking about a higher purpose although, certainly not ruling it out. A life of service is certainly significant and one of great joy. But for now, let's focus on having a great day, every day.

I wish for you that you too decide to surround yourself with people who lift you up.

I wish for you to recognise if a relationship, personal, working or otherwise is not serving you anymore, do something about it.

Something that was right yesterday, may not be right today. You may have changed, they may have changed, circumstances may have changed.

I wish for you to never be afraid of change

But also, be aware that this is not an excuse to be lazy. Life takes hard work. Pick a route and really stick to it. Or don't pick a route, just go where opportunities take you but don't use my words as a reason to never stick anything out. Hard work means commitment.

Relationships take commitment too, as much as I encourage you to be clear on what you expect from others, you need to take on board what they expect from you. If demands are justified and you fall short of them, apologise. No matter who they are and how far down the line you realise you need to, if an apology is really due, it is as much for you as it is for them.

Sometimes, it may be too late or too little. Even if you believe this to be true, and again if it is really due, apologise still. Never leave an apology unsaid, that can be a cause for future regret.

In fact, I wish for you to have the wisdom to never let a situation where something needs to be said, unsaid. My almost lifelong friend's father died suddenly when we were in our early 20s. We were all shocked and I thought to myself that she would be surrounded by people comforting her and I didn't want to disturb her unimaginable grief. So, I didn't call. I thought of her and her family constantly, my family and I sharing stories of him over and over. But I didn't call.

I thought it came from a good place, thinking, she is so busy right now, she won't want to speak to me. She knows where I am and that I will be here for her so she will call when she is ready to talk. But the older and wiser I am now, I know that even if it is the wrong time, saying the words means more than not saying them at all, even if not saying them comes from a good place.

I am not going to cry

In our list of bedtime phrases, you asked me to include: "I am definitely not going to cry." I went along with this initially, with an unease around it as I spoke. Soon, you asked me to drop the 'definitely', you couldn't explain why but you didn't want me to include that word anymore.

Your dad and I always stick together on our parenting approach, supporting each other in our choices and reactions, discussing differing opinions at an appropriate time. This said, there was always one topic we didn't agree on – telling you to stop crying.

I am wise enough to see that your dad's perspective comes from love. From his desire to protect you. Showing emotion, openly being vulnerable, these are not qualities aligned with strength and strength is a male's key attribute. In a world of equality, females too. Your dad's fear is that if you do not, at an early age, learn to control your emotion and hold back your tears, you will be seen as weak and picked on or bullied as a result.

This fear, I totally understand, I want to protect you. I want to protect you firstly from anything that may make you cry. Then from anybody that may tease you then from bullies and from the big wide world that can be a vast space of fear and the unknown.

But, if we stop you from feeling the emotions you need to feel, how will you know what you are capable of overcoming? How will you ever learn that tears stop, eventually and there is sunshine after the rain? And how will you learn that next time, they will stop quicker and then quicker still. How will you know the difference between emotions?

As you get older, I will be encouraging you to consider how long you want to feel this way. Acknowledging your emotions is one thing, but allowing them to take over is another. Putting the cause of the emotion into perspective is a skill that takes practice, the opportunity to practice though is the best way to learn.

A journey is a series of steps, it does not need a

destination

As well as the **_Sender Feels Better_** series becoming a wider purpose for me, it kick-started my love of writing, of sharing my message.

In publishing the books myself and trying to expand their reach, Sender has a life of his own with social media pages and his own website. Each week at least, I focus some effort into growing this idea. I have no end goal other than showing you that there are possibilities at your fingertips if you quiet your mind and follow your innate wisdom.

The words on the page didn't feel like they were mine, the idea came from my soul and the words fell onto each page and the series grew. I didn't have to find time to do this, I made time because I love it and it has nothing to do with money, it comes from passion.

So far, the books are selling, not enough for you to retire on yet and they may not sell a single further copy but I enjoyed every minute of effort and you also loved being part of creating these books.

Purpose becomes wider contribution

Like climbing a mountain starts with a single step and you normally cannot see the summit, the fog clears as you go. You may need to change the route you take to avoid an obstacle or for a simpler climb but that is ok, you will still ultimately get to the top. I have no destination for the Sender series but I have a weekly purpose to contribute to its growth, I may need to approach things differently sometimes and I may get things wrong but that is ok. I am enjoying taking the steps up the mountain of progress.

The same goes for life as a whole. Starting with an overall purpose of personal growth. On the days where no purpose comes to mind (and you will have days like these), choose a purpose of peace. A purpose of reacting to a situation or acting in the way that firstly brings you the most peace it can and secondly, is the most peaceful for all. What are you doing today to be the best and most peaceful version of yourself?

For me, by practicing more practical daily purposes, for example a specific focus like; writing more of a book or starting a certain task at work, I became highly-motivated and somehow found more time in each day. The more accomplished I became, setting my purpose became simpler, the consciousness of my purpose lifted and now my purpose is always peace, the action I need to take is instinctive.

It's also uplifting to realise that you can reinvent yourself everyday if you need to. You are under no obligation to be the same person you were when you were younger, or even 15 minutes ago. It's important to realise that who you were before and the decisions you made were right for you then, you made the decision you could with the information you had. With new information, even with new thinking, your decision may be different, and this is also fine. As long as you respect other people's feelings, fears and expectations and communicate as much as you can as often as you can, change is not bad.

In relation to my contribution, only now that I have a strong grounding, my core self, my heart, my soul, whatever you want to call it, can I truly and confidently expand my reach.

The wider a tree's roots spread through the earth to keep the tree steady, the taller the trunk can grow. The taller the trunk, the wider the branches can spread its fruit. Now that I have strength and purpose of my own, my own contribution

is intensifying.

And that is absolutely ok.

5 A life of SIGNIFICANCE

I wish for you a wonderful, joyful, fulfilled life. I wish that even though this will not always be the case, how you have been raised, the calmness in our home (except when you are wrestling or beating your dad at FIFA), has woven an inner peace within you that sets you up to take challenges in your stride.

I am also aware however that, influences are far more reaching than I have sight of and that, as life is like a game of snakes and ladders, it's our emotional intelligence that can predict how we weather the snakes we all inevitably face.

A player in the game of core wellbeing is significance. Yes, this can mean changing the world for generations to come, making an impact at a county, country, or even global level but it can also mean significance closer to home. You don't need to be on the international stage to hold significance, it can be as simple as a few words, chosen carefully.

When you understood what it meant, around the age of two and a half, you would love nothing more than waddling up to extended family members to tell them in your cute toddler tone:

"You're gorgeous." Seeing their faces light up, these two words, from you, made their day.

Words can stay with you for days, weeks or even longer. If they are unkind, they can significantly impact how you live your life.

I worked with somebody whose first language wasn't English. He was told in a meeting, many years ago, that his accent was: "Not easy to understand" and unfortunately, he carried those negative words with him ever since. In fact, he didn't speak up in meetings from that day forward.

The reality is, his English is incredible, better than some native English speakers, but even if it wasn't, his points and opinions are no less valid than anybody else in the room.

These simple unkind, throw-away words impacted his confidence and subsequently his desire to climb the career ladder. These words that stuck with him were from one individual, said to him once, a long, long time ago.

On the flip side, it's also true though that kind, positive words can have the same level of impact. They can build your confidence, resilience and even better, change your whole outlook - now this screams significance to me!

How good does it feel to receive a compliment? So now think, how good does it feel to deliver a compliment? Really knowing that the positive words you say will have a lasting and significant impact on the recipient and taking the time to build this into your day-to-day mindset can do wonders to your own wellbeing.

How often do you acknowledge somebody on a job well done? Or praise and give valid feedback on a report or presentation or to genuinely congratulate a win? Praise, credit, positive feedback -

it's free and quick for you, but has long lasting results.

I wish that your very nature is one of positivity and praise; however, in low times, instead of reaching for the wine or feeling sorry for yourself, an extension of hunting for help, to re-balance your state, is sharing a compliment. Going out of your way to lift the mood of somebody else, in turn lifts yours and fills your significance cup.

It can take as little as seconds out of your schedule so you cannot claim to not have time...Somebody you see, somebody you speak to, drop someone an email. Even better somebody you have bad energy with or somebody that you don't even know. Although, I also wish for you to have the wisdom to know when this could be seen as creepy!

Give them credit for something they did this morning, last week or even when you were a child. The positive energy this mindset of credit creates will come back to you in abundance, both in credit back to you and in the significance you feel in return.

Whilst these compliments may feed somebody else's need for external validation, they are ultimately harmless – you can't avoid spreading positive comments for the fear that you are fueling somebody else's misunderstanding. You can share in the hope that your words are taken as they are meant, a lighthearted lift in energy.

I had the pleasure of working alongside your Grandpa, my dad, in the early 2000s, he held a senior directorship but, despite his position, I was still regularly told what a gentleman he was. He is proof that it's not true that you have to be harsh, or stamp over people, to climb up the career ladder and he is also proof that just a few kind words from you can stick in someone's mind, they could even change someone's life...including your own.

Recognition from within

When you were in primary school, the teachers operated a system called the 'Golden Book'. This, in my opinion, highlights everything that is wrong with early year's education. Used as a tool to incentivise children in the class who needed to behave better, for those that didn't, it was a weekly cause of sadness. You didn't concentrate at school at this age, neither did I back then, and whilst, yes, there were definitely times you could have been more applied, it was not completely your fault.

Unfortunately, school wasn't engaging - learning was not made to be fun and aged four, five and six you needed more than you got – I am not surprised you were not inspired. But, you didn't act up, you just let your mind wander, resulting in less than A grade performance but no challenging behaviour that needed the carrot of a golden book award to bribe you by.

You were overlooked. Not put in the category of children that achieved what the school system classed as 'top marks' but, not at the bottom of the class either – somewhere in the middle that resulted in minimal appearances in this terrible book.

The trouble here was that you had, in your three years at this school, pinned so much adoration to this false accolade, you wished for a mention every week hoping that you had done something to catch a teachers' eye but, to our disappointment, your teachers were not looking at you.

What I wanted so badly was for you to see that you are already golden, on the inside, outside, in how you treat people, in how and who you are. No weekly list of repeated names changes that your core is instinctively kind and loving and thoughtful. You are also observant and smart and learn so fast. At the time of writing this, I hope that you will

soon see that other people's opinions of you do not equal your worth. You are, and everybody reading this is, unique and perfect, you don't need anybody else's gold star to prove this.

Your experience, your choice

I wish for you to impulsively sing loudly, breathe right into the bottom of your belly, laugh often including at yourself, move for joy not just exercise, love without expectation and forgive easily.

I wish for you to take everyday activities as a reason to feed your inner glow. Say 'thank you' even if the person you are thanking won't hear you. To hold the door open, yes, to be kind but, mostly for you, because it's kind and whether you get a 'thank you' or not is irrelevant, it says more about you than them. Wave thanks to a car that has stopped to let you pass even if it is pitch black. Be the person in the queue that lets not just one but two people in front of you, so what if it doesn't suit others, it's kind, and you are feeding your soul.

Following our release from one of the Covid-19 lockdowns, a neighbour's dog who had got used to her family always being around, became sad. After months of them being home every day, they started leaving for work again and it unsettled her, she became lonely and off her food.

I was still working from home every day and felt a bit the same, you were back at school and your dad back to work, I was home alone each day too so we came to an arrangement, Mini, the dog, would come to our house at 8am each weekday until her family were back from their day's engagements. They would provide her food and walk her before dropping her off in the morning.

Many expressed their surprise as this kind of arrangement

usually involved being paid – a dog sitting service for 8ish hours a day could be a good income! But it wasn't about money, ever. I loved having a dog in the house, so did you – we got company and doggy companionship from the relationship and Mini fast became one of our family, without the vets bills and we could still go on holiday anytime we wanted. If we started demanding money, our neighbours would've found another solution and we would've lost Mini from our lives.

Society may well think something should be done a particular way, but I wish for you that if a better way that doesn't fit the mold suits you better, go for it.

Please, don't be afraid to be different.

A home is a home is a home

Owning property is another example of society setting expectations. When I met your dad I was a serial renter. I had never owned a property and had no intention of shelling out the massive deposit / mortgage / maintenance costs to buy one. I had never had an issue with landlords, had freedom to move to where my life needed me to be or for the type of property I needed at that time. It worked for me.

Yes, many people told me: "Renting is wasted money" or "You are just lining the pockets of the already rich," but, I didn't see it that way. Things cost money, in this case, having a roof over my head, whoever owned it, cost money. I was happy to pay for that, also affording me the benefits of not being tied to one place, one building bought.

There is a modern fixation on owning property, often leaving those that cannot raise the capital feeling like they are missing out or lacking. There is also the fear of lost investment again leading to a feeling of missing out.

Property can also be volatile, and it isn't the only answer, investments come in all sorts of shapes and sizes as do happy homes. So what if your names are not on the property deeds, there are plenty of up-sides to not being shackled by a mortgage for 30+ years.

If not owning a long-term investment is an issue for you, but the first rung of the property ladder is out of reach, invest in something else exciting with a long-term goal in mind. Take advice, sure, but make it something you can get passionate about to turn a feeling of lack into one of optimism for your assets.

Remembering me

Equally grief comes with expectations. Dave Young, fellow Ultimate Coach Programme Alumni's wife passed away unexpectedly when their daughter was very young. I cannot speak for him but through conversations, I am aware of how our collective understanding of the power of thought turned his grief around.

Not everybody approved of his different approach, however the comfort that the approach we are now familiar with (3Ps) could give to many struggling with loss should not be dismissed.

I have no intention of going anywhere any time soon but, if I do, firstly, no need for a somber, sad funeral – scatter me wherever you and others close to me decide will bring you all peace. Please simply raise a glass (and a scone, cream first please) in my memory.

I hereby give you and anybody else reading this that knows me permission to smile, laugh, get on with living a positive life. I wish for you to never feel guilty for feeling hopeful or joyful when you think you should be mournful. In fact, it will be my greatest legacy if my passing does not cause you pain.

Sadness is ok, please let it flow, but more so remember our joy, our warmth and use it as a comfort. Miss me but I wish for it to not be in a way that creates a hole, I wish for you to find a way that spurs my love and my words to live on in you – remember...

"Snap"

If you need a helping hand to get to this place of peace with loss, I trust Dave to guide you. Seek him and take time to listen to his experiences, his ideas and his guidance.

6 A life of CONNECTION

Peace is the answer – always

Where an answer is yet to be found, only in peace of mind can the answer appear.

When you were 18-months, you went to a local nursery. You loved it there, you were confident and funny and kept everyone entertained. After a year or so, you started coming home with bruises. One day at pick-up, the team there told us that Henry had bitten you, teeth marks across your arms, you were in tears and I was too.

The next day, you didn't want to go but I had to work so reluctantly pushed you through the door. That night, you told us how it happened again, so I requested an explanation from the staff – how is this allowed to happen, one child singling out my sweet, calm boy?

We were not allowed to know the details of the incidents or even who the other child was, all we could go by was your daily recollection to us. You were nearly three, your concept of days and times was limited and although we were aware that your report of being hit again could have been a memory of the previous day, you are our precious boy and even one finger being laid on you was one finger too many.

The issue with doing something about it was that, I had no proof other than your reluctance to go back day after day so, with the team we agreed they would set up a diary, which was reported back to me each day so that we knew which days you were really attacked and which not – this sounds crazy even writing it now and it felt crazy back then, your dad was livid and convinced we should remove you from the pre-school completely but, we continued with the diary to understand the scale of the issue.

It worked out that this was three times a week occurrence but, there was a sudden change. You started to refer to Henry as your friend, you recalled games you played and ways you helped him. We now know that Henry is autistic and struggles to understand his emotions, you were caught in the crossfire for a short time but, once you realised, with the help of the nursery team, that he communicated differently and that he didn't comprehend things in the same way as you, you started to help him, almost becoming his protector.

One instance, you were sitting down for tea and the rule was that everybody had to be seated before the children could start eating. Henry tucked in before he was allowed and other children started to shout at him – you jumped in to defend him saying: "Henry doesn't realise, he doesn't understand like you. Don't shout at him, be kind" and you sat next to him to make sure he was ok.

I beamed with pride, and still do, at how you instinctively handled that situation. Nobody told you to look after Henry, especially as you had been on the wrong end of his emotions only days before. You showed innate kindness, a natural ability to calm and defuse conflict and to understand perspective and emotional reasoning, even when you are initially a victim – this quality is within you so here I am, reminding you that this is you, the real you before the world wrapped its roots around you and your protective guards grew to protect you from perceived threat and danger.

Because really, one thing I have learned myself and proven over and over in my life, is that with the exception of misaligned expectations which can mostly be resolved through clearer and more open communication, difficult and challenging behaviour nearly always comes from fear. Either your own or the other party. What are you afraid of that is causing you negative reactions, what are they afraid of that has prompted their walls to go up and they feel the need to protect themselves? This reaction could be in the language used or in the actions they take or don't take but I can almost guarantee you, there is fear at the root.

Lifting this theory up a level is the understanding that in life, most people really are doing their best. Their best to do a good job, to be the best version of themselves, to keep their heads above water. That said, fear is a natural emotion and of all the different characters that make up the world, their fear can mostly come from these four sources:

1) **Being taken advantage of**

2) **Loss of popularity**

3) **Change**

4) **Criticism**

So, in times of negative energy between people, I encourage you to remember who you were then, ok maybe not in real memories of that day but, who you are at your core, you are the kindness in challenging relationships, you are the protector when behaviours come from fear or lack of understanding. Before you react, please stop and think, what am I or what are they afraid of?

We all have a superpower

This leads me to the topic of anger. One of the four children's books in the series is called *Sender's Superpower.*

In this book, Sender understands that if someone raises their voice, it's not always because they are angry with the person they are shouting at. I wrote this book to empower the reader to understand that they are in control of their reactions. This has two initial layers:

How you react when you feel angry:

1) **If you feel angry and frustrated, that is fine, all feelings are valid. But how long do you want to feel like this?**

2) **What action can you take now to help this feeling subside?**

3) **What have you learned from this experience that gives you a greater understanding of your reaction to emotions?**

4) **How can you react differently next time for a better experience?**

How you react when other people direct their anger at you:

1) **When other people get angry, it may not be because of the person they are directing their anger at**

2) **Before you react back, what action can you take to**

understand where their anger is coming from?

3) If there is a valid reason for their anger towards you, what can you do to calm the situation, other than becoming defensive or aggressive?

4) If there is not a valid reason for their anger towards you, what can you do to calm the situation, other than becoming defensive or aggressive?

5) What have you learned from this experience that gives you a greater understanding of your reaction to other people's emotions?

6) How can you react differently next time for a better experience?

In times of anger, especially in children, this is a regular spot check;

o   Hungry?

o   Tired?

o   Afraid?

This is a valid list, for adults too, we all act differently with any of those three elements at play, but I challenge you to draw the list further asking yourself.

o   Do I want to feel like this?

o   Can I let this feeling go or does it serve me to hold

on to it?

Normally, by the time I get to the last check, I decide I can let this feeling go and move on with my day because I would much rather feel happy and content within myself than harboring a half-considered grump that will ultimately weigh me down. Heavy for a children's book, right!?

But not too heavy for this book because my wish for you is that you choose peace. We all have the capability, if only we attempt it, to tune into our emotions and decide for ourselves how we react. In building strong positive connections, being able to look beneath the surface reaction to a situation and consider underlying reasons can be enlightening. For ourselves, being alert to our behaviour is the first step in building our emotional intelligence and considering an appropriate response – in my opinion far more important in life than academic intelligence.

This does not mean that injustice should be excused, if you are genuinely being taken advantage of, pull the ripcord. If, however, reactions are at a superficial level and letting go of ill emotion will ultimately clear the way, being the bigger person feeds the soul. It is totally natural to feel angry at times, but it is never ok to be mean.

I am not a textbook academic, I wasn't engaged at school, my grades were not impressive, I was far more interested in the social side of life than learning. I have theories on that now, especially as I watch you go through our limited, short-sighted, misdirected education system, but two things; I am more than clever and smart when it comes to getting things done and I am emotionally intelligent. I understand myself, my feelings, my reactions and triggers and I understand how I can get the most out of my experience.

I believe the saying: 'You get what you are.' You, at your core innate self as you proved throughout your childhood. Please never forget, you are kind, caring, funny and smart. If you continue to be this person, without walls or masks or restrictions, you will, I am sure of it, attract the same people to come into your life.

The key, I promise you, is peace.

David taught me that comparison is the thief of joy

The first of the **Sender Feels Better** series of books I wrote, the one that fell out of my head first is called **Sender Chooses Fun.** Written as my way of trying to help you handle losing, the book focuses on Sender, mistakenly believing that he has to win at everything. This misunderstanding is fueling his behaviour.

Losing makes Sender so miserable that his friends don't want to play anymore. Not only is it not fun for Sender but it is also not fun for them. Around the middle of the book, the text reads 'he notices he is sad either way, alone or playing just to win'.

Sender recognises that focusing 100 percent on winning, no matter what the cost, isn't actually that much fun at all. It is even worse when his friends don't want to include him anymore.

This book is designed to sow the seed that focusing on misunderstood beliefs, may be impacting our own ability to enjoy our journey. Believing we have to look a certain way to be respected or earn a certain amount of money to fit in, or even that crying is a sign of weakness can fuel limiting behaviour.

I wish for you to see that we are the masters of our own experience, we decide how we feel. Not some old-fashioned principle, or a misunderstanding about how we will be accepted in society. As long as your actions are not at risk of causing harm or of breaking the law, our actions are our decisions too.

Inner Connection

Before you joined our family, I had a business idea. It was a good idea and I maintain that. I also had a good idea about how to structure the startup of the business and get the idea to market - I maintain that was a good idea too, perhaps even better than the business idea itself.

I am many things but an action taker, much to your father's frustration, is top of the list. So, I set about initiating launch plans, engaging with the people I needed to join me on this adventure and getting paperwork in place.

It picked up momentum and with the newly assembled team and in parallel to developing the product, I was preparing customers, even taking early orders.

The costs of setting this up were high and it was self-funded with additional in-team investment, so it was risky, but I had faith in the idea and structure so spent weekends and evenings pressing forward.

I'd commit time to my paid contracts by day and work on this project at night, handy as the early enrollees were in opposite time zones.

But, I admit, I made a mistake.

I took my eye off the ball, distracted by the pressure of the financial balancing act launching a new business can be, I went against my instinct, I shut out my wisdom and I made a bad choice.

I can see my error now, with clarity and perspective. I didn't know to trust myself. I can also see that in making this bad choice, I let down those around me. It didn't end well and for that and the impact it had on those involved, I am truly sorry.

I felt ashamed and guilty and, once the business had dispersed, I recoiled. If I had that time again I would have communicated and behaved differently. I understand that my reactions came from my own fear, but I won't and I cannot hold onto my mistake like a weight.

I immediately directed my energy elsewhere, determined not to get off the treadmill - my fear was being branded a failure but a failure I now know I was not. There is no treadmill other than the one you imagine in your mind.

It didn't work out, many businesses don't - I'm still ok.

My car was hit side on by a land rover with roll bars. Despite my injuries - I'm still ok.

I've had my heart broken, I've lost money, I've missed planes, I've been late for meetings, I've been stuck in traffic, I've had applications rejected, I've lost friends. I've made mistakes - I'm still ok.

Ups and downs are part of the journey. Watch any Disney movie and you will see plots full of false starts, rock bottoms as well as feel-good highs. Listen to any Disney song and you will hear lyrics of resilience, healing and learning how to play the game of life.

Because it is a game and if you don't shoot, you are guaranteed to always miss.

Knowing things may go wrong doesn't excuse overt risk taking or disregarding consequences though and I trust you to follow your wisdom to make good choices.

You are already so wise

One of the Three Principles is 'mind'. This refers to the 'universal mind', that presence of a wisdom likened to gravity. It's always there, barely questioned but protective by its very presence if only you are open to listen.

Roald Dahl wrote: *'Those who don't believe in magic will never find it'*, it's the same for wisdom. If you are prepared to trust it, like a faith we all have wisdom within. Consider tuning into it like learning a new language or skill in that it may not appear easy to comprehend at first but, like faith that we are where we are meant to be or setting boundaries for our inner toddler, if it is not natural to you keep practicing, the skill will get stronger with every attempt.

Your instinct, intuition, impulse, these are all wisdom. Trusting that very first spark in your gut, before you put all the doubt and overthinking around it, that is listening to your wisdom.

My wisdom and yours are different - ours are different to you, your dads or our neighbours. What is instinct for you may be opposing to mine but that is good, yours is right for you and it is why I cannot tell you how to act in situations or guide you to a decision. I can offer my view as 'your mum' but, you should be free and feel valid enough to go with your own intuition.

The thing with wisdom though is that it needs space, it needs a place to formulate, to communicate to you in its own way. An iceberg tip full of comparisons and challenges, resentments and goal seeking is too full to allow wisdom in.

Wisdom already knows the lessons you have committed to your berg beneath the waves, it considers the unnecessary niggles you have already cast out to sea. What it presents to you, in your peaceful quiet mind is your truth, your answer, your compass. Not mine or the shopkeepers or the hairdressers but yours and the more peaceful your mind, the more wisdom can expand.

With this 'in mind' when invited to offer others guidance, the best route to answer it is to help them to calm the noise and slow the speed of their thinking, in turn helping them to find their own wisdom.

This may sound at odds with the sentiment of this book. In some pages, I share my advice rather than just the tools I offer to slow your thoughts. However please know, I have no expectation that you follow this way, I just wish for some of these pages to filter through and, should you ever need it, for you to take solace from this understanding.

Reflecting now, I'm glad the business didn't work out. I would have been responsible for supporting global infrastructure, on site during the Covid-19 pandemic when the world shut down. I can't imagine that the income for the early employees would have been enough to support expansion 'in country' and with travel restricted, we would have been in a more than tricky position.

There are still reasons this business I dreamt up would have flourished though but in moving on, I focus on what serves me.

One day you, your dad and I were walking in a car park. You spotted a car that was an odd colour: 'Is that car yellow?' you asked. I thought it was more green and your dad agreed with me but, there was no harm to anybody or to yourself in you choosing to call it yellow, because it was your favourite colour and seeing it as yellow made you smile.

Where do you think the title of **_Sender sees Yellow_** came from?

7 A life of **GROWTH**

Mostly my career has brought me joy. I love the purpose that work brings, the achievements and challenges to navigate. Between the ages of 23 to 28 I worked for a company that made products used by the parcel delivery industry. Initially working across the UK, my role was basically sales. I had increasingly fancy titles but the simple truth was it was my job to generate the business more money.

The company was small which meant a small team so once the customer had agreed, I was also responsible for making it happen. The product was technical, and I am good with technical detail. I can also assess reactions and adapt to the energy in a room. More than this though, I understand people, pitching my waffle just right to seal many deals. The role required me to present to audiences, some small but very senior – heads of large businesses and huge budgets. Some audiences were large but less high-brow, training engineering teams on how to use the kit.

When my employer eyed international expansion, I was chosen to lead the department, a department of one – me. The world was my oyster and with them covering the expenses, I lived it up! I pitched to audiences across the globe from Finland to Singapore, from Saudi Arabia to Lithuania.

I had no fear…"Bring it on" I would say. Even though I mostly travelled alone, I made memories, learned of different cultures, met incredible people and awed at the world's wonders.

I always tried to keep my track light and add humour where I could. I would shoot from the hip with little structure, but mostly always managed to get my point across. On occasion, I would need to present through an interpreter. It was always funnier for me though when the point of my quip was lost…waiting for the room to snigger, only to be met with tumbleweed – jokes don't always translate well but, I still laughed at myself!

A company sale, float on the AIM market and an accusation of smuggling into Russia later, I moved on. I set up on my own as a consultant and despite my spiral, I have not looked back, I've always loved independence and the role I do now, at the point of writing this book, could not be more perfect for me.

But in between it all, at a point I cannot recall, I lost my nerve. I began to fear the audience. My relenting confidence started to wane and a piece of who I thought was me fell away.

My confidence was tested, my voice would shake and my cheeks flush. My heart would race and on occasion my mind would go blank. I could still hold a room 1-2-1 or 1-say, 10. But give me a room full of eyes staring at me and I wasn't myself anymore.

Later down the line, when I realised that investing in myself was not selfish, that my own path and growth is just as important as anybody else's. I also love to learn so I signed up to be coached in public speaking. It surprised me that I, an international speaker, needed this course but I did and this stuff really works. Whilst I come so much more from a position of being yourself, knowing what you should say in that very moment, I also know that practical knowledge is, in the right setting, equally as important.

You don't just get on a bike and know how to ride. Doctors don't know how to treat patients instinctively. Knowledge can be committed to our intellect, we don't need to reference it every time the need arises, doctors don't refer to their study books in every consultation, nor do drivers have the highway code in front of them for every journey. You can rely on knowing what you need to know in the moment but, in most instances, you need to know it in the first place.

The following guidance not only applies when speaking to a crowd but also when approaching a situation you are nervous about like a job interview, your first day in a new job or a difficult conversation. This can even apply to just being confident in 1-2-1 discussions.

Stand up for yourself – standing up when speaking, holding an open pose with chin high will instantly lift your confidence.

In a room where everyone around the table has to introduce themselves, even if everybody remains seated, I still stand up! I remain confident, and often stay remembered.

Dress it up – wear clothes that are appropriate to the occasion, better still, wear attire to one level smarter. Ensure they are well pressed, shoes shined. Whilst your message is far more important than your appearance, feeling the part is about your confidence level, nothing to do with your audience's opinion. They are going to judge you regardless but if on the inside, you feel polished and professional, it will lift your soul.

What you have to say is important - your words, views and opinions are just as important as the next person's. Nobody is more or less important than you. In society, we put people on pedestals, but they are the same make-up of biology, but with differing vision, hope, ideals and we approach things in different ways. We can all learn something from everyone, and you absolutely deserve to be having this conversation.

Be clear but don't raise your voice – speak slowly and clearly, keeping your chin up to project. There is evidence that if you lower the inflection of your voice at the end of a sentence, it generates more trust, and you gain credibility in your words. The opposite is raising your voice at the end of a sentence which sounds more like a question, like you are asking yourself if what you are saying is true.

Timing matters – yes, be early, but also set some time aside to plan and practice what you are preparing to present. Time your delivery, splitting your content into three sections, start – tell them what you are going to be telling them. Middle, tell them. End, wrap up, repeating the key points. Watch the news and see how they do it; you get the headlines, then the actual news, then the and our 'main story again.' This format has been a winner since news began.

Go easy on yourself - your existence is not resting on this one conversation. Your worth is not attached to the next 30 mins. Although it may feel like it, your path should it not go the way you believe you want it to, will ultimately go the way it should. You may not get the job, land your message, get the sale but, you will be ok. You will get what you need when you need it. Who knows, there may be a bigger, better opportunity just around the corner, you just are not ready for it yet.

Substance-v-style – I found it interesting to learn that there are two types of speaker; a dog and a cat. A dog is seeking validation, speaking quickly, like a puppy panting. Fitting multiple topics into a short pitch, tail chasing information where the overall outcome is to be adored. The cat however is an independent force, the point is to be heard, unashamed if they are not loved in the process. Selecting a few topics to present but each one is well covered and reinforced with no detail missed.

Pick your style and base your structure on it – do you want to put lots of information into your communication and allow your audience to fill in the gaps or is it better in the scenario you are focused on to narrow the subject but cover it thoroughly? Don't be afraid to switch styles in different situations.

Select powerful language – somehow, the language we use daily has become apologetic. Often sentences are started with: "Can I just say…?" or "I am sorry but…" or delayed emails are opened with: "I am sorry for the delay" or closed with: "Does that make sense?" For your message to be received as strong and believed, skip the back foot language. Instead opt for: "Thank you for your patience" or offers of further correspondence should the recipient need it, not automatically assuming that your words are not full and explanatory.

And finally…Don't let fear stop you from sparkling, your sparkle may be subtle at first, but it is still a sparkle, it will get shinier with time. My voice still shakes but it doesn't stop me from speaking.

I know my mind and now I speak it, at work I am bold. I have difficult conversations. But, I try not to argue for arguing sake, I hope to consider that my position comes from one of knowledge. Nowadays, I also try to take into consideration the other parties' position more, realising that usually there is fear involved.

I have difficult conversations because I remove the emotion from it, it's work, this is not my everything, I am more than just this. My level of consciousness is higher than the emotion that could be attached to these words. I try not to be rude, but I set my purpose. I am assertive and I choose my battles, I don't cry wolf and up the ante if I don't feel necessary, aiming to only progress if I am clear on the outcome I need to achieve, and it is possible to achieve it through this means. If it is not a possibility, preserving my peace is always the priority.

Where difficult conversations do take place, try not to hold a grudge. Move on with peace in your mind. Grudges do more to weigh down the person carrying it than they do to prove a point to the person it is held against. Holding onto ill feeling, even for injustice way in the past, serves little purpose, they are unlikely to be aware, nor will it impact their actions. My advice is to let it go. Commit the knowledge to your intellect, remember your experience and protect yourself from it happening again but any ill feeling should float off on the sea of waves surrounding your iceberg.

You see, the thing about the past is it's only a snapshot of memories your mind has created. I shared the introduction of this book with my parents before it was finalised and they both commented on the piece I wrote about my dad's New Year's resolutions. Their memories and mine were different, recalling dad's annual recital as: "Be happy". My memory remains the same, your Grandpa said: "No regrets." This is ok, we recall moments differently and hold the picture we have painted ourselves as our truth.

The real truth, however, lies somewhere between your picture, other artistic recollections created and the weathering of time.

I once read: "It's never too late to have a happy childhood" and this is true of any past phase, even particular jobs. I hope you have had a happy childhood but, for those who have not, re-read that sentence again please and consider the position of your camera lens.

Take work in your stride

I wish for you to remember that the boring, annoying parts of working life are just stepping stones, it can't always be fun, fun, fun. The same goes for your experience. Living your life at this base level is surrendering to a life of frustration. Some stuff, we just have to do, no amount of overthinking will change it and if you cannot change it, you are wasting energy letting it into the tip of your iceberg.

Like the point behind the Sender book ***Sender Sees Yellow,*** we all have the same view from the window. We can choose to just see the fog and rubbish bins or we can look through them to the trees and blue sky.

I have already pointed out, you were not a big fan of early-years learning, and I understand that. You were never difficult but would regularly repeat how much you hated school. We went through terms, when Covid-19 didn't interrupt your attendance, of your sunken shoulders, dragging your heels on the way down the alley. But I realised, if you had fun activities to look forward to at the end of the school day, you cared less about the 9-3 boredom. So, I scrambled play dates and clubs into at least three weekdays – this changed your mindset, you couldn't go to an after-school club if you didn't first go to school!

Money talks?

Money also has no emotion attached to it, many people fear talking about money because we have been taught by society that money is bad, wanting more money is greedy. If you feel like you always want more, you are coming from a position of lack, a position that ultimately will not provide abundance.

For some, seeing others splash the cash can stir up unhealthy emotions, judgement, comparison, jealousy. I have witnessed many a 'just look at them, jetting off on another fancy holiday!'

tut. I don't doubt that I have been guilty of more than one of my own green-eyed stares.

There is an old theory that money goes to money…. or does it?

In recent years I have pondered a less crude outlook: What if money goes to a money mindset? Or instead, what if growth goes to a growth mindset and income is a welcomed by-product of personal progress?

Directing any energy towards the judgement of others' success, questioning their flashy choices; disappointingly comparing any financial deficiency to their flowing abundance feeds your feeling of not having what you need.

I wish for you to consider feeling happy for your successful neighbour or genuinely congratulating your colleague on their bonus win - and ending your opinion there, with sincerity. Instead of judgement and competition, return your energy inward. Focus it on commitment to your own growth, prepare for your own career journey, develop your own skills and don't be afraid of self-investment.

After all, what is success anyway? They may actually hate holidays and crave family time at home but feel desperately anxious by the pressure of keeping up appearances? Having it all, doesn't always include happiness.

Your value doesn't come from what you have, it comes from who you are and what you put out into the world. If that is dedication, positivity, and belief that what you *need* will come, your lack can shift into your own abundance.

Smart talking

Most of my career highs have been the result of previous

connections I've made, like meeting the BBC radio producer, I have very rarely sought out a new role and been through an application process, in fact I don't ever remember doing so from my 20's onwards.

I wish for you to make connections, to be remembered for your contribution and your soul and for this to serve you as well as doing the same for me.

I also hope that you build an awareness that silence can be as important as words. You don't always have to have an opinion, deciding not to get dragged into other people's business, work or not, can be calming. Not every conversation at work or home serves you, choosing not to say anything is also, in this situation, choosing peace. I am not saying sit there with a blank face, unresponsive but excusing yourself is perfectly ok, better still, it is emotionally mature.

An extension of this is knowing that 'no' is a full sentence. In many situations you do not need to explain your reasoning for opting out. If saying no feels right, do so without fear of judgement, you need say no more than that.

Silence is also perfect for calming your mind. Where an answer is not forthcoming, a busy mind full of seeking and overthinking cannot form new ideas. Slow down, make space in there for your wisdom to appear.

Maintaining humour where you can, even through an interpreter, can also be emotional maturity. Not taking yourself too seriously is a way of building resilience. Things don't work out frequently, this is part of life, the more you are able to laugh at life's ups and downs, the higher your consciousness will carry you, and ultimately, I believe the lighter you will float through with ease.

Sharing is caring

I wish for you to be the energy, to light a room instead of dim it. Sharing your low mood can bring others down too.

There are opposing views on the Covid-19 situation and I try to view each side from a position of knowledge, rather than emotion. Reading to understand but making my own decisions. My decisions being what I feel is best for me (and those I input) at that time, considering peace too but still challenging where I felt necessary and not being led by others' individual choices.

During the Covid-19 lockdown, in a time when schools were still open, but we were not allowed to socialise (unless your name was Boris), the only human interaction we had outside of our home was when dropping you off at school. Overall, we coped pretty well during the many lockdowns, our calm home stayed so and we took on new activities such as chess and making cardboard castles so my mood remained buoyant apart from the odd frustration and missing family of course.

One morning, I passed another parent who shared her opposing mood with me, fed up with the situation and desperate to be set free, she off-loaded her dissatisfaction and I soaked it all up. Walking away I felt like permission had been granted for me to despise my own situation too, I went from feeling pretty ok with it all, just concentrating on the peace in my own bubble to bursting that bubble and taking on the frustrations of the nation.

Once my bubble burst, in the instant that it took, I felt low, angry, hard done by, victimised and proceeded to have a bad day at work, actually more than one bad day and fed my low mood in my habitual way.

When I reclaimed my power over the mood, I realised I had taken on somebody else's problem, I didn't use my own position to analyse the situation. I was fine, in fact so was she, she had just chosen to fill her tip with the different side of the coin to me.

I am absolutely not saying don't air your view or speak your mind, I absolutely encourage that, your view and opinion are as important as everybody else's, however, remember misery loves company.

8 Take-Aways

Firstly, here are the basic checks to bring to your focus should you feel off balance:

1) **Recognise that thought is the route of our experience**
2) **Nobody is broken, sometimes we can get stuck in a misunderstanding**
3) **If clearing your mind to allow space for wisdom does not come naturally, start by filling your iceberg tip with joyful thoughts**
4) **Hold off on decisions until any low mood has passed**
5) **There is no need to try to hunt for an answer, the answer is already within peace of mind**

Now, here are the take-aways I most wish for you to commit to your intellect. The stories, journeys and connections are part of our path but the knowledge I have taken from this is important for me to share with you. I hope you may choose to share it in your own way too.

The easiest way I can describe my understanding is by asking you to visualise layers. Self-built layers that cover our core or heart or soul; the protection, the thick skin, the misunderstandings, the masks and pleasing of others against our own wishes. Each layer could be formed of:

- Critical or negative inner voice
- Over-thinking
- Over-sensitivity
- Needless worrying
- Excessive perfectionism
- Excessive judgement of yourself and others
- Guilt
- Shame
- Regret
- Paranoia – imposter syndrome
- Self-criticism
- Deep routed disappointment

Take your pick, I am sure there are many more. The more there are for you, the further from a peaceful core we become. The further from our soul we are, the more challenging we find our experience.

Can you hear the alarm bells?

I believe we have an inner warning system; sadness you cannot shake, long-lasting low moods, over-nervousness (any low mood feeling that doesn't actually need a label) all tend to be the early indications and if we don't hear them and try to clear the layers that have distanced us from our souls, this clever warning system will sound louder. Anxiety, depression, panic attacks. If we still don't listen, perhaps attempting to drown out the alarms with alcohol, overeating, controlling behaviour, other vices, our system has no choice but to throw us some physical signs.

This is not the root of all physical issues, genetics, biomechanical issues and many other reasons however, what little I do know, from research and experience, I believe that these signs can be sent to sound our alarms louder. To warn us that we have too many layers and we have ignored the signs for too long. The further from our souls, the harsher the sign. The more we have been trying to drown the warnings, the louder the warnings become.

I am not ready to write about pain. My journey of managing pain is on-going, suffering I think as a result of the car crash that altered my late teenage years. That said, I see the truth in pain being alert and absolutely believe in the connection between mind and body. Embarrassment causes my cheeks to flush, nerves my heart to race. So why not connect more deeply to our personal situation or outlook? Louise Hay makes the connection between ear pain and words we do not want to hear, back pain and a feeling of not being supported, leg pain and not wanting to move forward in the current direction.

Wider than this though, I wish for you to take each warning as that, a reminder to remove the layers. No need to press too deeply into why the warning happened, save your energy for what comes next. I believe that the reason the warning finally got your attention, isn't the reason you feel the way you do, it could be all the misunderstandings before it that lead for the final band to snap. The reason I spiraled was not because my hair was falling out, it was because the years prior to this bizarre, unexplained allergy changed the way I live. I had forgotten that I am important. This forgetfulness does not make me a victim, nobody is to blame, I just forgot. But, now I remember, I wish for you to always know, so you never get the chance to forget and never get too far from your core.

Through society, the press, and social media, we think we are feeding our souls through food, alcohol, relationships, material belongings, chasing success, and online attention. This is what advertising, brands and 'influencers' want us to believe too. What we are really doing, beyond basic need, is pushing our truth further away. The simple reality is, the closer to our souls we are, the more we are at peace.

For me, my core is my heart, and my layers are elastic bands and when I lost my way, I was the furthest from my heart I had ever been. My heart was covered in so many bands I couldn't see through them to make my way back. The bands were so thick that the next band's stretch to reach all the way around was too much for it to bear and it snapped. Instead of the straw that broke the camel's back, this was the band that snapped me.

My warning signs started with overthinking, fear of judgement, stress, anxious feelings. Next my signs were panic attacks, paranoia, which I drowned out with bad habits. I didn't know to listen, so I missed the signs. The warning got louder and I was warned with a sudden burning allergy, melting skin and clumps of hair all over the shower tray.

I cannot even recall what that last band was, which is evidence in itself that the ultimate action was irrelevant, but I certainly heard the alarms then and my transformation began.

My heart could be your soul, your core or tree trunk. My elastic bands could be your bandages, plasters? It could be flames or lava. For me, my bands were all based on my misunderstandings;

- **I have to be seen to have everything under control**

- **If I lose everything, I will never get it back and I will have failed**

- **I make so many mistakes, I can't be good at anything**

o I need to be busy to be significant

o I can only be happy if everybody else's needs are met

o I am only valuable when I am serving others

o My worth is based on what other people think of me, including my appearance

o Other people are so much better than me

o How other people behave towards me is what I deserve

o My mood is decided by what is going on around me and other people's behaviour

o The voice in my head is always right

o I don't deserve to do well

With the feelings being attached to these misunderstandings feeding my negative state leaving me:

o Too busy
o Stressed
o Tired
o With bad habits

o Listening to my unkind inner voice
o Overthinking situations

Throughout this book, I have written for you. I have tried to impart my experience in the hope that you can gain some insight into what makes me tick, but to also guide you to make balanced choices. Of course, along the way you will make mistakes, we all do and that's part of the huge learning curve. Now though, my bands are gone, replaced with clear protective casts. Protecting my core is their purpose and they represent the pillars I maintain through what I have introduced to you in these pages.

If in doubt, always remember;

1) **Security** – knowing that you will be fine, regardless of the situation and that you are exactly where you are meant to be is enough

2) **Adventure** – laugh, don't take your thinking too seriously, make your own way, realise it is all a game, the snakes are as important as the ladders

3) **Purpose** – concentrate on finding your own inner peace, then your purpose. Your wider contribution will be an extension of this, with a strong core will ensure your wider reach does not dilute from your inner calm

4) **Significance** – live with that purpose, be the energy, make a difference, say the kind words that will make your day, making somebody else's at the same time. Most of all, choose peace

5) **Connection** – surround yourself with good people, not being afraid to walk away when it is wrong but investing your energy when it is right, trust your wisdom to know the difference

6) **Growth** – learn, push your comfort zone, meet fear with action.

My darling Sebastian, I believe that if I still didn't listen, my warning system would have kept trying until I finally did, it could have got much worse. I wish for you to know that if you ever get far from your soul, the guidance in this book will get you back there. Think of it like this, if you are running around fretful and anxious that you have lost your keys, it is not because of your keys.

.

9 Bibliography

Below is a list of books I recommend for various situations. It is also the source of much of my learning, I just joined the dots for myself.

For everyday life:

- The Inside Out Revolution – Michael Neill

- Somebody Should Have Told Us – Jack Pransky

- The Power of Now – Ekhart Tolle

- The Courage to be Disliked - Fumitake Koga, Ichiro Kishimi

For grief:

At the point of writing this book, my fellow Ultimate Coach programme Alumni and advocate of the 3Ps is also writing his own. Having lost his wife at an early age, David Young has an alternative approach to grief that I trust and should you need it, please seek him out and be open to his words.

For relationships:

    o   The Relationship Handbook – George Pransky

Energy, physical wellbeing:

For trusted guidance on physical wellbeing including nutrition and energy, please seek: Anna Anderson

Pain:

    o   You Can Heal Your Life - Louise Hay

    o   If you have physical pain, please again seek trusted

        fellow Ultimate Coach Dawn Rothwell

What would mum say?:

If for some reason I am not here, longer term and you want to seek what guidance I would give in given situations, ask your dad and sisters of course, then also seek trusted guidance from Anna Anderson and Rachel McGarrigal.

Reference:

The titles of my chapters and within the take-away's chapter are my interpretations of Tony Robins presentation of the 6 core human needs; **Certainty:** assurance you can avoid pain and gain pleasure, **Uncertainty/Variety:** the need for the unknown, change, new stimuli, **Contribution:** a sense of service and focus on helping, giving to and supporting others, **Significance:** feeling unique, important, special or needed, **Connection/Love:** a strong feeling of closeness or union with someone or something, **Growth**: an expansion of capacity, capability or understanding.

Printed in Great Britain
by Amazon

85441112R00058